BY NATIONAL BEST SELLING AUTHOR

Casandra Johnson

Remember

Back

in the Day

FOREWORD BY
DR. MYLES MUNROE

AFTERWORD BY ERIC JEROME DICKEY

Remember Back in the Day

Remember Back in the Day

Complete with Memorable Moments That Helped to Shape Us
PLUS
A Bonus Cookbook with Recipes from Grandma's Kitchen

BY NATIONAL BEST SELLING AUTHOR
CASANDRA JOHNSON

FOREWORD BY
DR. MYLES MUNROE

AFTERWORD BY
ERIC JEROME DICKEY

Updated and Revised

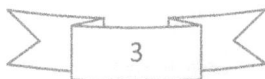

Casandra Johnson

Cover Design by: Brand[U] Inc., www.branduinc.com
ISBN: 978-0-9827001-1-2
Printed in the United States of America.

Published by: Kingdom Journey Press, Inc. –
A full-service publishing company,
www.kjpressinc.com

Casandra Johnson

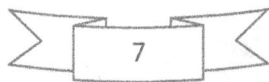

Remember Back in the Day

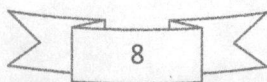

Dedication

"Remember Back in the Day" is dedicated in memory of my late grandmothers, Mrs. Dorothy Mae Leasley Barnes and Mrs. Julia Johnson, and my godmother and aunt, Ms. Georgia Johnson, and as a tribute to my mother, Ms. Lizzie Johnson, my daughter, Ms. Brittany Hemphill, and future generations yet to be born.

Remember Back in the Day

Acknowledgements

First and foremost, I thank my Heavenly Father and my Lord and Savior, Jesus Christ, Who is the Author and Finisher of my faith. It has been quite a journey, but I thank You for Your Holy Spirit which has kept me, and for trusting me to walk through it so that I may be fit for the call and assignment that You have given me for Your Kingdom!

To my mother, daughter, sisters, nephews, and nieces – Thanks for hanging in there with me through the good, bad, happy, and sad!

I shall always honor and appreciate the memory of my late father, Mr. Issac Johnson, Jr., for giving and speaking life to me before his transition.

To Dr. Myles Munroe – What can I say? I am certain the Holy Spirit commissioned our paths to cross after the passing of my natural father, which was during one of the most critical hours of my life. Thank you for praying for me and answering the call from God Himself to speak into my life as a father does.

To Dr. Benson Karanja – Thank you for taking the journey from Kenya to the Office of the President at Beulah Heights University. My life has been forever changed as a result of your leadership and wisdom. Thank you for also believing in me to get the job done!

To Pastor Riva Tims – God divinely ordered our steps to meet during the summer of 2006 at the Prime Meridian Restaurant in Atlanta. Because He is all knowing, I am certain that He allowed us to reconnect for a time such as this! You are truly a jewel!

To Eric Jerome Dickey – From one best-selling author to another - thanks for all that you do and for paving the way!

To Johnnie Williams – We shall always remember, as well as impart, the wisdom and memories we received from the back in the day which helped to shape us.

To one of my dearest and closest friends on this side of Heaven, Prophetess Sonobia Parker – Some people come into your life for a reason, and some for a season, but I thank God for sending you for a lifetime. You are truly a friend who has stood closer than a sister or brother. To you and Evangelist Anita Myles – How can two (or three) walk together except they agree? The pact we made stands yesterday, today, and forever more!

To my school mates from back in the day while attending various schools in Washington, DC and Prince George's County, MD during the 70s and 80s - Leckie Elementary, Owens Road Elementary, John Hanson Junior High, Oxon Hill High, and Crossland High – We were among the generation who witnessed the beginning of the crisis leading to the senseless bloodshed of many of our young brothers and sisters

To Kita Williams of Brand U Inc. – Thanks for all you do to help make it happen!

To all of my co-laborers in ministry – Let's remain true to God's Word and that which He has called us to do for the sake of His Kingdom!

There are many others where it would take another book for me to acknowledge all of you. Know that I appreciate everyone who has come into my life because everyone of you has been absolutely essential.

Casandra Johnson

Remember Back in the Day

Casandra Johnson

"Remember Back in the Day" was inspired by a conversation with a stranger at the Publix Grocery Store on Cascade Road in Atlanta, GA as we were at the deli counter waiting to place our orders. When the clerk arrived, the other lady at the counter requested an order of bologna, and that's when it all began.

Remember Back in the Day

Table of Contents

Remember Back in the Day

Casandra Johnson

Remember Back in the Day

Foreword by Dr. Myles Munroe

This erudite, eloquent, and immensely thought-provoking work *"Back in the Day"* gets to the heart of the deepest passions and aspirations of the human heart. It proves that no matter how big a tree grows of how many Fruit it might bear; it can never outgrow its root. This book is about the value and indispensability of original foundational principles of life. This work should be required reading for anyone who wants to live life above the norm. This is a profound authoritative work which spans the wisdom of the ages and yet breaks new ground in its approach and will possibly become a classic in this and the next generation.

This exceptional work by Casandra Johnson is one of the most profound, practical, principle-centered approaches to this subject of foundations I have read in a long time. The author's approach to this timely issue brings a fresh breath of air that captivates the heart, engages the mind and inspires the spirit of the reader. It proves that no matter how much man may advance or progress, there are principles and precepts we can never out grow.

The author's ability to leap over complicated theological and metaphysical jargon and reduce complex theories to simple practical principles that the least among us can understand is amazing. This work will challenge the intellectual while embracing the laymen as it dismantles the mysterious of the soul search of mankind and delivers the profound in simplicity.

Casandra's approach awakens in the reader the untapped inhibiters that retard our personal development and her antidotes empower us to rise above these self-defeating, self-limiting factors to a life of exploits in spiritual and mental advancement. We must protect the foundation if we want the house to have value. The author also integrates into each chapter the time-tested precepts giving each principle a practical application to life making the entire process people-friendly. Every sentence of this book is pregnant with wisdom and I enjoyed the mind-expanding experience of this exciting book. I admonish you to plunge into this ocean of knowledge and watch your life change for the better.

Dr. Myles Munroe
BFM International
ITWLA
Nassau Bahamas

Casandra Johnson

Remember Back in the Day

Casandra Johnson

Introduction

Progression is advantageous; therefore I dare not suggest we return to everything we used to do "Back in the Day". I do however recommend we take a moment to remember what actually worked to help shape us and build strong families, communities, and churches.

I was born in 1969 in Gulfport, MS, almost one year to the day after Dr. Martin Luther King, Jr. was assassinated. My parents were born and raised in Mississippi, however they moved to Washington, DC in 1968 to provide a better life for their children. While I have never lived in Mississippi, my mother believed what many young women did back then and that was, she felt it necessary to be with her mother as she was bringing her newborn baby into the world. As a result, she returned home for a brief period when it was near time for my delivery in order to be with her mother for her wisdom, guidance, and support.

I have two sisters, one older and one younger. Although we lived in the city for practically all of our lives, our parents passed down values from their upbringing in the south, as well as we learned from our neighbors, whom many of their families were also originally from the south. You see, during the era when I was growing up in the 1970s, our neighborhoods were a community, or "village". As a matter of fact, I remember some of the different communities and developments actually including the word "village" in their names, therefore this was the type of upbringing my sisters and I came to know and understand.

When I was a young child, everyone knew each other in the neighborhood and helped to raise one another's children. Our communities included everyone from family members, neighbors, preachers, teachers, politicians, policeman, and even the owners and employees of the local corner stores, who played an active role in raising the children in their neighborhoods. They all took a vested interest in ensuring the neighborhood was safe and the children grew up to make something of themselves. Their philosophy was each new generation was to become better than the last. During that era, we knew and respected the people in our neighborhood, and collectively we represented a family unit.

While my generation was blessed to experience the village, we also had the misfortune of witnessing the ball being dropped somewhere during the late 1970s to early 1980s timeframe. As a result, future generations after us experienced something totally different, which has now brought about devastating consequences in our society.

I began wondering whether anyone else from my generation noticed what had taken place. In asking this question, I had the opportunity to speak with Johnnie Williams, a young man who was born just two years before me and raised in Los Angeles, CA. Our paths crossed some 40 years later in Atlanta, GA where we had the opportunity to dialogue about how it use to be back in the day. Although we hailed from opposite sides of the country, he from the west coast, and I from the east coast, our fond memories of what it was like back in the day were very similar. Johnnie and I also agreed that times have drastically changed from when we were growing up.

Johnnie Williams and I were both products of single parent homes led by mothers who had no choice but to work in order to provide for their children. Our era signaled a time when divorce started to become commonplace and tear families apart. In spite of being left alone to raise their children, our mothers were strong in their faith and did their best to instill spiritual and moral values in us.

Johnnie and I also understood the concept of what later became known as latchkey kids, which are children who are given the keys to come home after school without any adult supervision. The difference from when we were growing up was our mothers knew they could depend on neighbors to watch out for us while they were working. We also knew we had to come straight home after school and have our homework completed before our mothers came home from work. Something has drastically changed however where it's no longer as safe for children to be given the keys and be left alone while their parents are working.

Some examples of what it was like for us growing up back in the day was if something suspicious was going on in the neighborhood, there were neighbors who were watching. If the children were doing something they were not supposed to, the neighbors would not only tell our parents what we were doing and who we were doing it with, but they also had permission to get us too. There was no such thing as strangers in the neighborhood because everyone was known by name, which made it easy for the neighbors to identify them. Now days, we call people like this "nosey neighbors", but these same type of people were both necessary and well respected back in the day.

On the other hand, if we were bold enough to cut school, we knew we could not go home, and we also knew we could not freely roam the streets or go into local establishments during school hours. The reason was the teachers would call our parents, the neighbors were watching, the truancy officers were out policing the area, and the business owners and employees would not allow children to enter their establishments during school hours. If any adults for that matter saw children out during normal school hours, they would immediately stop and say something to them. With all this to consider, we knew it was in our best interest to just go to school. In today's society however, children can cut school and practically no one will say anything, and while there are kids who come home after school without adult supervision, statistics show this is the time when they are at a much greater risk of getting into trouble.

Our families, communities, and churches are now in a serious state of crisis whereby many of our children born after the 70s era cannot fathom or relate to what we experienced in previous generations. Why? Because something has been lost in the transition and we now find ourselves in a state of emergency. As an overall society, we have moved so far away from many of the essential norms which helped to bring our ancestors over, thereby creating a crippling effect that has diminished our sense of spiritual and moral values.

While there is a sense of relief that we have moved forward in many areas, there are a lot of things we once did that were good enough for our grandparents and parents, and perhaps still good enough for you and me too! Because of the crisis we now face, it seems logical, and also vital that we take a journey to reflect, and perhaps even chuckle, on some of the things we used to do "Back in the Day" that actually worked to build strong families, communities, and churches.

Enjoy the Journey!

Casandra Johnson

Remember Back in the Day

1

That's My Mama

Mama was off the chain "Back in the Day"! From head to toe, she stood tall, never failing to display her quiet strength, beauty and grace. While she exhibited the most radiant smile, she was also powerful. She could just look at her children and they automatically knew what to do!

In today's society, we often look to various mediums to gather vital information and developmental tools, however I recall a time when the most valuable life lessons came from experiences which took place right in our home. Many of them were derived from the things mama used to say, and do, which helped to mold and shape us.

Even when faced with the most difficult challenges of life, Mama maintained the where with all to rule her home well. She kept everything in control and her children reverenced, obeyed, and called her blessed. Not only was she skillful in setting the tone for her house, but she also set the atmosphere for the entire community and made everyone feel like they were at home!

Home

In the hit movie "The Wiz", Stephanie Mills performed a song entitled "Home" where there is one stanza in particular that stands out to me, which says:

> *"When I think of home,*
> *I think of a place where love is overflowing*
> *I wish I was home, I wish I was back there*
> *With the things I've been knowing"*

"Back in the Day", I knew home to be a place that was built on a foundation of love which started with Mama, the matriarch of the family, and the entire neighborhood. Back then, the African Proverb which states "it takes a village to raise a child" stood true. Her wisdom was sought after, her love and gentle warmth admired, and her food devoured because it was absolutely scrumptious.

Everyone on the block knew, loved, honored, respected, and obeyed Mama as if she were their own! At least this is how I knew it to be during the era when I was growing up.

When I think of home, I think of the communities I once knew where everyone came together like family, even in the inner city. Home for me was our Nation's Capital and its surrounding suburbs where there were not only historical landmarks such as the White House, Monument, Capitol, and various museums, but there were also communities built by families that were just as, if not more, beautiful. Back in the Day, we knew, understood, and valued everyone and everything that made up our neighborhood.

While I do not suggest we revert to everything we once did back in the day, there are some fundamental qualities and characteristics from my upbringing that can be identified with the place I called "home". Thanks to Mama and everyone who made up the village, I knew home as a beautiful, exciting, and safe place "Back in the Day"; and this is the environment I long for my children and future generations to experience!

Do You Remember the Times 3

When I was growing up during the 1970s, everyone in the neighborhood knew each other and helped to raise one another's children. Our communities included everyone from family members, neighbors, preachers, teachers, law enforcement officials, politicians, and even the owners and employees of the local corner stores who all took a vested interest in ensuring the neighborhood was safe and the children grew up to make something of themselves. Their philosophy was each new generation was to become better than the last. During that era, we knew and respected the people in our neighborhood, and collectively we represented a family unit.

While my generation was blessed to experience the village, we also had the misfortune of witnessing the ball being dropped somewhere between the late 1970s to early 1980s timeframe, which has brought about devastating consequences in our society. As a people, we have now moved so far away from many of the essential norms which helped to bring our ancestors over, thereby creating a crippling effect that has diminished our sense of spiritual and moral values.

Because of the crisis we now face, it seems logical, and also vital that we take a journey back in time to remember, and perhaps even chuckle, on some of the things we used to do "Back in the Day" that actually worked to build strong families and communities.

Enjoy the Journey!

Casandra Johnson

Those Who Learn Teach

"Your job is to speak out on the things that make for solid doctrine. Guide older men into lives of temperance, dignity, and wisdom, into healthy faith, love, and endurance. Guide older women into lives of reverence so they end up as neither gossips nor drunks, but models of goodness. By looking at them, the younger women will know how to love their husbands and children, be virtuous and pure, keep a good house, be good wives. We don't want anyone looking down on God's message because of their behavior. Also guide the young men to live disciplined lives."
Titus 2:1-6 (The Message Bible)

There is an African Proverb consistent with this passage of scripture which states "He who learns, teaches." Back in the day, the older people understood the importance of teaching the younger people by their words and actions; and the younger people listened to and respected the older people, regardless of whether they were their parents or not. It is because of these truths that our communities were once stronger and better, however the unfortunate reality is, somewhere and somehow, something has changed.

Back in the day, we taught our children how to love, and not hate; how to give, and not take; how to build, and not tear down; how to be a friend, and not an enemy; how to communicate face to face, and not through cyberspace. We were kind, we were patient, we were personable, and we kept our word. We laughed together, cried together, played together, prayed together – we were unified in the home and community.

It is now time that we reunite as a people to teach the younger people the critical and essential norms which were once good enough for our grandparents and parents, and perhaps still good enough for you and me.

It's Training Day

Train up a child in the way he should go: and when he is old, he will not depart from it.

Proverbs 22:6

I recently had the opportunity to re-watch the movie "Training Day" which was released in 2001 and starred one of my favorite actors, Denzel Washington. I watched the entire movie twice within a few days time span, which I did not quite understand why at the time, but now it has become perfectly clear to me.

In the movie "Training Day", Denzel played one of the leading roles as a corrupt cop named Alonzo, which is unlike roles he is typically known for playing. Oddly enough, out of all the incredible leading roles Denzel has played in past movies, he won his first and only Academy Award to date for Best Actor in a Leading Role for the part he played in this movie.

While I must agree that Denzel no doubt goes over and above to play all of his characters exceptionally well, what stands out is he won an Academy Award for a role portraying corrupt behavior as a law enforcement official, which was once a career viewed by society as honorable. In addition, he also terrorized a community of people that had become riddled with corruption, drugs, and crime. He was in turn honored and recognized with one of the highest awards in the land for a role that represented the worst type of behavior, which ultimately led to his violent death in the movie. While there is a spiritual message in the movie based on Romans 6:23 which states "For the wages of sin is death; but the gift of God is eternal life through Jesus Christ our Lord", the unfortunate reality is this movie portrayed how many communities have actually become.

The village has been lost and it's time for the very people who make up our families, communities, and churches to take their rightful place and pick up the ball from where it was dropped. There is still a vibrant generation among us who remembers what it was like to grow up in the village, and we must take the time to remember, and also train the younger generations that came after us. It is possible to take our families back because the Bible tells us in Philippians 4:13 that "I can do all things through Christ which strengtheneth me", and in the words of our 44th President of the United States, Barack Obama "Yes We Can"!

There is still hope, therefore it's time for the older people to once again begin training the young by giving them examples, sharing their stories, and providing them with recipes to live by for the soul, mind, and body.

As you now begin turning back the pages of history, I invite you to "Remember Back in the Day" when....

Casandra Johnson

Remember Back in the Day

Remember Back in the Day When

Faith

We believed in the One and Only true and living God and did not use His name in vain.

The Bible was reverenced by men as Holy.

Attending Sunday school and worship service was not an option, but a way of life.

We understood God had no respect of person; therefore we did not either.

Families prayed and read their bibles together.

Children said their prayers before going to bed at night.

People gave thanks to God before eating.

Prayer was accepted in schools.
As a result, schools were safe.

The pastor knew everyone in the congregation by name and even ate Sunday dinner with the members.

We respected preachers as God's messengers and therefore believed what they said.

When preachers traveled out of town for ministry engagements, they stayed in the homes of members from the host church.

The Ten Commandments was one of the premier television movies.

The pastor's lifestyle was representative of the congregation they led.

Churches had buses and vans that went into the neighborhoods to bring families who did not have transportation and children to service.

We felt the presence of God in our churches, homes, and communities.

Believers were not afraid to confess their faith in public settings.

The foundation of the state was the church.

There was no such thing as being politically correct.

The altar and everything in and around the church was recognized as Holy Ground.

People of faith strived to live a life that was pleasing unto God, both in public and private.

People of faith knew and understood their God given authority and walked in it accordingly.

We were led by the Spirit of God in what we did so that He would be glorified, not by what would bring us fame and fortune.

The world looked to the church as an example and not the other way around.

People studied the Bible for themselves and had the ability to rightly divide the truth.

There were church mothers who were allowed to speak up when people got out of line, including the preachers if they misinterpreted the word of God.

There was a clear, visible distinction between the church and unchurched.

Ladies dressed modestly and did not wear clothing that exposed their private body parts.

People came to church to worship God and not a man or woman.

People saw the church as a place of worship and not a place to seek business opportunities.

Family and Home Life

Mothers were viewed as family matriarchs.

Fathers were viewed as the head of household and breadwinners.

Mothers could just look at their children and put the fear of God in them.

Today, children look at their parents and put fear in them, and that's not God!

Mothers would press and curl their daughter's hair, and not allow them to use chemicals until they were at least young adults.

Young girls were not allowed to get their hair cut.

Afros were in style for men and women.

My most distinct memory of afros during my era was The Jackson Five and Thelma Evans from Good Times.

Home Economics was a required elective class during junior high, or secondary school, where one semester included cooking and the other semester included sewing with real sewing machines.

A sewing machine, needle, and thread were household items.

At least one person in the family knew the phone numbers by memory or had it written down for close relatives, distant relatives, neighbors, and friends. For every number they did not know, there was a phone book from the telephone company nearby that had the phone numbers listed.

Today, many people do not even know their own telephone numbers by memory, let alone anyone else's. We have become a society that relies on cell phones and computers to store phone numbers and if they crash, all contact is potentially lost.

We gave our children names with meaning and that were easy to spell, pronounce, and also transcended across generations.

Saving for our children's future was more important than spending hundreds of dollars in the here and now or on designer clothes and shoes.

There was no such thing as designer clothes and shoes, but children wore what their parents could afford or what their older siblings grew out of and passed down to them.

Parents raised their children.

Children honored, respected, and obeyed their parents.

Children did not talk back to their parents.

Children, young and old, feared their parents almost as much as they feared God, if not more.

Mother was home to prepare a hot breakfast before the husband went off to work and the children went off to school.

Mother prepared Sunday dinner on Saturday night so the family could sit down and eat right after church service.

Parents would literally wash their children's mouth out with soap if they said a bad word, which sometimes was not even really a bad word, but it was considered offensive or disrespectful.

In our house, the word "lie" was considered as a bad word. My sisters and I never said that word in the presence of our mother until we were well into our adult years. I still hesitate in saying it even today.

Children had household chores which did not just consist of making their beds.

We could not go to bed unless the kitchen was clean.

The kitchen was not considered clean unless all the dishes were washed and dried, the stove and counter tops were cleaned, and the floor was swept and mopped.

We were our brother's and sister's keeper.

Family members were there for each other. For instance, if a family member wanted to move to a new city where other relatives lived in order to get a new start in life, the family in that city would receive them by making room and also helping them find employment.

In today's society, many family members barely even speak to one another and jobs are few and far between.

Marriage was honorable and considered as the true definition of a covenant relationship.

Marriage was between man and woman.

Husbands and wives fought for their marriage and would hang in there with each other for better or worst.

Families gathered for more than weddings and funerals.

Families ate meals together at the table.

If children did something wrong, they would get the whippings of their lives and it was not considered as child abuse. And guess what, they still turned out ok.

During a lightning storm, we turned off all lights, unplugged electrical appliances, and the entire family took cover together in one room.

Mother could prepare a full meal out of what appeared to be little to no food. Not only was it enough for the family, but some of the neighbors would also come by and eat too.

Mother cooked and baked from scratch without using measuring spoons.

Young girls watched as mother cooked and learned how to prepare full course meals before reaching teenage years. If mother had to work, dinner was prepared by the time she made it home.

We bought whole chickens from the grocery store and cut them up into parts.

We bought ground beef and made home-made burgers from scratch with chopped onions and green peppers.

Children believed they could be anything they dreamed of being.

A big highlight for kids was getting to the bottom of the cracker jacks box for the prize.

Cereal boxes also had prizes and siblings had to rotate on whose turn it was to get the prize.

We made bologna sandwiches by taking the red wrapper from around the edge, fried it in the pan until the center rose up and it was slightly burnt around the edges, slapped cheese on top of it, and then put it on bread with mustard.

We popped popcorn on top of the stove.

We made home-made popsicles out of kool-aid.

There was no such thing as microwave meals.

We packed food and snacks for road trips that included items like fried chicken, sandwiches, potato salad, chips, fruit, and sodas.

Eating out at McDonald's and other fast food restaurants was a treat and not a way of life.

We witnessed Barack Obama become elected as the first African-American president of the United States of America

Friends and Community

We greeted people when we passed them by.

It was normal to have conversations with total strangers.

"Drugs" was a term used for medicine prescribed by a doctor and filled by a pharmacist.

The younger people automatically knew to offer their seat or place to the elderly or disabled.

Men and young boys offered their seats to women and girls.

Teachers played an active role in the children's lives and well being.

For instance, if a child did not show up for school, the teacher or school called to find out where they were, or if a child acted out while in class, the teacher had the authority to discipline the child and also contact their parents to receive the support they needed.

Neighbors knew each other and would call the parent if they saw the children doing something out of line, like skipping school.

Truancy officers patrolled the streets during school hours and if they saw children, they picked them up and took them to school.

————————

We had neighborhood block parties with food, games, and music to bring everyone in the community together.

————————

Families were not quick to move from the neighborhoods because they served as a since of community where everyone looked out for one another.

————————

We offered a ride to someone we knew who did not have transportation or even to total strangers.

————————

Teachers were respected because we knew they were vital to the success of the family and community.

Adults were always right and children did not accuse them of not telling the truth.

————————

The younger people sat at the feet of the older people to hear stories such as about the times when Dr. Martin Luther King, Jr. was alive.

It was considered gross for young boys and girls to touch or kiss each other.

We had compassion for others when they were going through a difficult time.

If an adult or elder person walked up as a conversation was taking place that was not respectful or pleasant, the conversation would cease.

Our word was our bond.

At least one house in the neighborhood was designated as the community house where all the kids came to hang out and have fun, and the mother in that house was like the other children's mother.

A friend would stick closer than a brother or sister.

Friends would dress in the same outfits and share clothes with each other.

Children respected anyone who was an adult.

The elderly, preachers, teachers, and law enforcement officials were highly respected.

The younger people listened to the older people to gain wisdom, knowledge and understanding.

We knew our neighbors by name and had conversations with them.

Children did not know the first names of any adults, especially teachers. They were all addressed as "Mr. or Ms." and their last name.

It was not out of the ordinary to borrow items like sugar and flour from our neighbors and when we did, it did not become the neighborhood gossip.

People came together to have rent parties because they cared enough for their neighbors not to see them lose their homes.

If we were poor, we didn't know it.

If there was a single parent or less fortunate family in the church or community, or if someone lost a loved one, everyone came together to assist them during their time of need.

If children had an argument or fight, they quickly made up and started playing together a few minutes later, as if nothing ever happened.

In today's society, too many of our children are losing their lives due to senseless violence as a result of arguments over minor issues.

There were working pay phone booths on the street corners, at gas stations, and at local establishments, along with telephone books.

We did not use cell phones as a primary telephone, especially when there was a working landline phone available and within reach.

We communicated with others by either calling them on the phone or going to their house to visit.

Today, communication has become impersonal where we rely heavily on computers and text messaging.

We gave driving directions based on the public transportation routes.

Remember Back in the Day

The punishment for misbehaving in school was to stay after and wash the chalkboards or write "I will not talk or misbehave in class" 100 times.

———❧———

We stayed and retired from the same career and organization we started with after completing high school or college.

———❧———

There was such a thing as retirement and pension funds.

———❧———

We had to punch in and out on time clocks.

———❧———

We used shorthand, dictation, typewriters and landline telephones.

———❧———

We used adding machines and dot matrix printers.

———❧———

Teachers stayed after to help children who were struggling with school work.

———❧———

Teachers taught students how to solve math problems by hand, the long way, before teaching them the shortcut or how to solve them by calculators.

———❧———

We went to the local corner store to buy real ice cream.

———❧———

I am now reminded of this with one of my newfound favorite ice cream shops named Kilwin's.

There was no such thing as lactose intolerance, therefore it was ok to eat and drink dairy products.

It was ok to drink water from the faucet and outside water fountains.

The ice cream trucks sold ice cream and candy.

The kids would sound the alarm so that everyone in the neighborhood knew when the ice cream truck came on their street.

Fun and Entertainment

Children's cartoons, television shows, and movies were really made for children.

We used a wire hanger as an antenna for the television.

We used the dial on the television to manually change the channels.

There was no such thing as a remote control for televisions.

Today if we can't find the remote control, we will spend an enormous amount of time looking for it, versus using the manual control buttons on the television to change the channels. If it is determined that the remote control is lost, we will even go as far as to abandon use of the television all together or go out and purchase a new remote control or television.

Mother would call the children from the opposite side of the house to change the television channel.

We watched television shows that were appropriate for children like The Flintstones, the Jackson Five Show, Good Times, The Jefferson's, The Brady Bunch, Mister Rogers' Neighborhood, What's Happening, Leave it to Beaver, and The Andy Griffith Show.

The neighborhood children came together to play games like tag, basketball, cheerleading, double dutch, hop scotch, jacks, and hide and seek.

We caught lightening bugs and ladybugs for fun.

There were only 5-7 major television networks. For us it was ABC, NBC, CBS, FOX, UPN, PBS, and WDCA-Channel 20.

We used street lights as a clock to know when it was time to come in from playing outside.

Children would take almost anything they could find to use for fun and games and make the best of it, like water hoses connected to fire hydrants to cool off on a hot summer day or boxes to make sleds on a snowy day.

We motioned our arms to acknowledge truck drivers when riding on the highways and also as a way of asking them to honk their horns.

We could access television stations without cable and all of the channels would sign off no later than two am in the morning.

***

There were no sexual scenes or profanity aired on television or radio stations.

***

We had record players.

***

We had 8 track tapes and wax albums.

***

Music had meaning and did not degrade women or a race of people.

***

We could understand the words used in rap music.

Casandra Johnson

Remember Back in the Day

How On Earth Did We Get Here?

"Our Father, which art in heaven, Hallowed be thy name.
Thy kingdom come. Thy will be done in earth, as it is in Heaven.
Give us this day our daily bread.
And forgive us our debts, as we forgive our debtors.
And lead us not into temptation, but deliver us from evil: For thine
is the kingdom, and the power, and the glory, for ever, Amen."

Matthew 6:9-13

As I was in the final stages of completing the manuscript for "Remember Back in the Day", I had the opportunity to attend an in-studio recording session with the sensational gospel duo, Mary Mary. Someone later asked what it was like for me to spend time with them.

While I have been in different settings before with Mary Mary (whose real names are Tina and Erica Campbell), on this particular occasion we were in a small, intimate studio environment. Not only was I able to enjoy their ministry of music, but I also had a chance to observe them up close and personal as they interacted with one another as natural and spiritual sisters. For me, it was an absolutely inspiring and life changing experience that could not have come at a more perfect time. My reply to the question was

"They are jewels and represent the epitome of a genuine relationship between sisters that is to be emulated."

I submit to you that something has been lost in our families that have also spilled over into our communities. It is as if the very fabric of our foundation has become unraveled to the extent that we are now in need of a skilled seamstress to mend the stitches that once knitted us together as a people. There has been a breach whereby never in the history of mankind have people been so cold, corrupt, and distant from one another. This should not however come as a surprise or mystery because of what was written in the Bible thousands of years ago in 2 Timothy 3:1-7 which states:

> [1] *"... that in the last days perilous times shall come.*
> [2] *For men shall be lovers of their own selves, covetous, boasters, proud, blasphemers, disobedient to parents, unthankful, unholy,*
> [3] *Without natural affection, trucebreakers, false accusers, incontinent, fierce, despisers of those that are good,*
> [4] *Traitors, heady, highminded, lovers of pleasure more than lovers of God;*
> [5] *Having a form of godliness, but denying the power thereof: from such turn away.*
> [6] *For of this sort are they which creep into houses, and lead captive silly women laden with sins, led away with divers lust,*
> [7] *Ever learning and never able to come to the knowledge of truth."*

We are indeed living in perilous times and because of the current state of the world in which we live, I believe humanity has grieved the heart of God. It's not so much driven by those who are not spiritually grounded, but more so as it relates to what has even crept into our churches. This by no means is intended to bring an indictment against the true and living church as established by

God, because His church is still alive and well. It is however intended to sound an alarm that the earth is out of alignment and now is the time for the saints of the Most High God to rise up and be accounted for and become the people and church that God has ordained for us to be.

He that has an ear, let him hear what the Spirit of the Lord is saying to the church.

It's sad to say, but we are now living in a time where people have become lovers of themselves. It even goes as far as there are some whom men and women have begun to esteem and worship as if they are greater than God and His word clearly tells us in Exodus 20:3 that "Thou shalt have no other gods before me". It's for this reason that the church now stands at a critical point of decision where we must choose who and what image we are really promoting. Will the real church please stand up and be an example to those who are living in a lost and dying world?

I suggest to you that today is a day of repentance, as we are living in a day and time where people are hurting like never before, not so much at the hands of the world, but some of it is even at the hands of what is happening in the church. As the world faces some of the most difficult economic times in history, now is the perfect time for the church to rise up and take their rightful position of authority and provide the answers the world needs, not the other way around. The problem however is families within the church are falling apart at an alarming rate, even among the highest levels of leadership. Many churches have also become so disjointed and are too busy fighting among themselves, thereby rendering it close to impossible for us to come together in a unified manner in order to have a major impact which brings about positive change in our society. Because of this, the church is no longer viewed by the masses as a place of safety, or where people have confidence in who we are and what we are supposed to stand for. We are the only examples of Christ that many may ever see and I am sad to say that too many have misrepresented His name. Instead an environment has been created where people have become lovers of themselves, the divorce rates are at an all time high (of which I must admit that I too have played a part in this), that is conducive to cliques and social clubs, and people who look down on others because of what they think a person may or may not have, therefore failing to recognize that the people we turn our backs on may be the very ones who God has sent as an angel of light.

The very foundation of who we are as a people was built upon our obedience and faith in the One and Only True and Living God, who has provided us with the framework to live by in His Holy, Inspired Word. He is The King of Glory and desires to dwell among you.

Casandra Johnson

Remember Back in the Day

Recipes for the Soul

And the LORD said unto Cain, Where is thy brother Abel? And he said, I know not: Am I my brother's keeper?

Genesis 4:9

THE TEN COMMANDMENTS

Thou shalt have no other gods before me.
Thou shalt not make unto thee any graven image, or any likeness of any thing that is in heaven above, or that is in the earth beneath, or that is in the water under the earth;

Thou shalt not bow down thyself to them, nor serve them; for I the Lord thy God am a jealous God, visiting the iniquity of the fathers upon the children unto the third and fourth generation of them that hate me; And showing mercy unto thousands of them that love me, and keep my commandments.

Thou shalt not take the name of the Lord thy God in vain; for the Lord will not hold him guiltless that taketh his name in vain.

Remember the sabbath day, to keep it holy. Six days shalt thou labour, and do all thy work; Bu the seventh day is the Sabbath of the Lord thy God: in it thou shalt not do any work, thou, nor thy son, nor thy daughter, thy manservant, nor thy maidservant, nor thy cattle, nor thy stranger that is within thy gates: For in six days the Lord made heaven and earth, the sea, and all that in them is, and rested the seventh day: wherefore the Lord blessed the Sabbath day, and hallowed it.

Honour thy father and thy mother: that thy days may be long upon the land which the LORD thou God giveth thee.

Thou shalt not kill.

Thou shalt not commit adultery.

Thou shalt not steal.

Thou shalt not bear false witness against thy neighbor.

Thou shalt not covet thy neighbour's house, thou shalt not covet thy neighbor's wife, nor his manservant, nor his maidservant, nor his ox, nor his ass, nor anything that is thy neighbors.

Exodus 20:3-17

And if it seem evil for you to serve the LORD, choose you this day who you will serve; whether the gods which your fathers served that were on the other side of the flood, or the gods of the Amorites, in whose land ye dwell: as for me and my house, we will serve the Lord

Joshua 24:15

If my people, which are called by my name, shall humble themselves, and pray, and seek my face, and turn from their wicked ways; then will I hear from heaven, and will forgive their sin, and will heal their land.

2 Chronicles 7:14

He who spares his rod [of discipline] hates his son, but he who loves him disciplines diligently and punishes him early.

Proverbs 13:24 (Amplified)

A merry heart doeth good like a medicine, but a broken spirit drieth the bones.

Proverbs 17:22

He who finds a wife finds a good thing and obtains favor from the Lord.

Proverbs 18:22

———————◦•●•◦———————

A man that hath friends must shew himself friendly: and there is a friend that sticketh closer than a brother.

Proverbs 18:24

———————◦•●•◦———————

Train up a child in the way he should go: and when he is old, he will not depart from it.

Proverbs 22:6

———————◦•●•◦———————

He that oppresseth the poor to increase his riches, and he that giveth to the rich, shall surely come to want.

Proverbs 22:16

———————◦•●•◦———————

Can two walk together, except they be agreed?

Amos 3:3

My people are destroyed for lack of knowledge.

Hosea 4:6

Man shall not live by bread alone, but by every word that proceedeth out of the mouth of God.

Matthew 4:4

It's more blessed to give than to receive.

Acts 20:35

Three things will last forever-faith, hope, and love-and the greatest of these is love.

1 Corinthians 13:13 (New Living Translation)

Be not deceived, God is not mocked: For whatsoever a man soweth, that she he also reap.

Galatians 6:7

And let us not be weary in well doing: for in due season we shall reap, if we faint not.

Galatians 6:9

Study to shew thyself approved unto God, a workman that needed not to be ashamed, rightly dividing the word of truth.

2 Timothy 2:15

Your job is to speak out on the things that make for solid doctrine. Guide older men into lives of temperance, dignity, and wisdom, into healthy faith, love, and endurance. Guide older women into lives of reverence so they end up as neither gossips nor drunks, but models of goodness.   By looking at them, the younger women will know how to love their husbands and children, be virtuous and pure, keep a good house, be good wives. We don't want anyone looking down on God's message because of their behavior. Also guide the young men to live disciplined lives.

Titus 2:1-6 (The Message Bible)

Now faith is the substance of things hoped for, the evidence of things not seen.

Hebrews 11:1

Beloved, I wish above all things that thou mayest prosper and be in health, even as thy soul prospereth.

3 John 2

Remember Back in the Day

9

Recipes for the Mind

A family that prays together stays together.

Prayer changes things.

Respect your elders.

In God We Trust.

Practice what you preach.

American Proverb

In prosperity, our friends know us; in adversity, we know our friends.

John Churton Collins

Mind your manners.

We are blessed to be a blessing.

He who learns, teaches.

African Proverb

It takes a village to raise a child.

African Proverb

Casandra Johnson

Knowledge is power.

Francis Bacon

What would the Jesus in you do?

Casandra Johnson

The way to a man's heart is through his stomach.

English Proverb

Remember Back in the Day

Recipes for the Body

10

Back in the day, eating out was considered a luxury or treat, and not a way of life. You see back then, mama, or big mama, would throw down, even sometimes making a meal out of what seemed to be a little bit of nothing. As it turned out, not only was it enough for the family to enjoy, but the neighbors somehow found out and also came by to take part!

Back then, young girls also came into the kitchen while mama was cooking to observe and even help out with preparing the meals. It was during these moments that many young girls learned how to prepare a full-course meal, even before reaching their teenage years. I personally found there to be something interesting about the whole kitchen experience and that was, while mama was cooking, she somehow managed to miraculously keep the house intact. Not only did she cook, but she also washed dishes, cleaned the counter tops, stove and floors, and even talked on the telephone and kept the children in line, all at the same time. By the time she was finished preparing her meal, the house was intact because she was skilled at multi-tasking and was the master of her kitchen and her home!

Somewhere along the line, something has been lost and we now have many young ladies, many of whom now have children of their own, who have no idea how to prepare basic food dishes. Because it is necessary for us to eat in order to survive, and it's also not wise to eat out every day, it's vital that we teach our young ladies, and men, how to prepare some of the very basic recipes from grandma's kitchen.

Let me first caution you that since we have now become a more health conscious society and food is not made and processed the way it used to be back in the day, it may not be wise to serve some of the recipes provided here on a daily basis. What you will find however is while many of our recipes as presented have evolved over time in an effort to create healthier meals, they still take on the resemblance and taste of dishes prepared right in grandma's kitchen.

Bon appétit!

Casandra Johnson

Recipes From Grandma's Kitchen

- ➤ Spaghetti with Meat Sauce
- ➤ Lasagna
- ➤ Fried Chicken
- ➤ Baked Chicken or Turkey Parts
- ➤ Barbeque Chicken
- ➤ Salmon Fillets
- ➤ Salmon Croquettes
- ➤ Sautéed Spinach
- ➤ Spinach Salad
- ➤ Tossed Salad
- ➤ Sautéed Asparagus
- ➤ Collard or Turnip Greens
- ➤ Green Beans
- ➤ Macaroni and Cheese
- ➤ Mashed Potatoes
- ➤ Potato Salad
- ➤ Scalloped Potatoes
- ➤ Sweet Potatoes
- ➤ Yellow Squash
- ➤ Homemade Burgers
- ➤ Homemade French Fries
- ➤ Fried Bologna Sandwich – One of my favorite classics!
- ➤ Fresh Squeezed Lemonade
- ➤ Sweet Iced Tea with Lemons

Each recipe is designed to serve 4-6 people

Spaghetti with Meat Sauce

Ingredients
1 lb pack of Ground Turkey or Ground Beef
Pack of Italian Sausage Links (Optional)
1 small Green Pepper
1 Small Onion
6-8 Fresh Mushrooms
6 oz can of Tomato Paste
15-16 oz can of Tomato Sauce
16 oz box of spaghetti
Vegetable Cooking Oil – 1 tablespoon
Salt
Pepper
Lawry's Seasoned Salt
Garlic Salt

➢ Cook ground turkey or combination of ground beef and chopped Italian sausage (only need 1-2 links) in a skillet on stove top over medium heat
➢ Add dash of salt, pepper, seasoned salt, and garlic salt to meat while cooking
➢ Add chopped green peppers, onions, and mushrooms while meat is cooking and stir ingredients together
➢ Crumble ground turkey or beef while cooking
➢ Cook meat completely through until brown
➢ When meat is completely cooked, use a drainer to remove excess oil from the meat
➢ Put meat back in a skillet and add can of tomato paste, tomato sauce, and water (12 oz to 1 cup), adding another dash of salt, pepper, seasoned salt, and garlic salt
➢ Cover with top and continue cooking on low for 30 – 60 minutes

- ➢ While the meat sauce is cooking, boil water in a saucepan and add 1 tablespoon of vegetable oil
- ➢ Once water begins to boil, break spaghetti in half and add to the water
- ➢ Allow the spaghetti to cook until soft
- ➢ Once the spaghetti is cooked, use drainer to remove water
- ➢ You can either combine the spaghetti with the sauce or keep separate and serve spaghetti with meat sauce on top
- ➢ As a short cut, substitute Ragu Spaghetti Sauce in place of the onions, green peppers, mushrooms, tomato paste, tomato sauce, and water.

Recommend serving with Spinach Salad or Tossed Salad and Texas Toast

Lasagna

Ingredients
1 lb pack of Ground Turkey or Ground Beef
Pack of Italian Sausage Links (Optional)
1 small Green Pepper
1 Small Onion
6-8 Fresh Mushrooms
6 oz can of Tomato Paste
1-15-16 oz can of Tomato Sauce
1-8oz bag of Grated Mozzarella Cheese
1-8-oz bag of Grated Cheddar Cheese
1 box of lasagna 16 oz – will only need about ½ the box
Vegetable Cooking Oil – 1 tablespoon
Salt
Pepper
Lawry's Seasoned Salt
Garlic Salt

- Cook ground turkey or combination of ground beef and chopped Italian sausage (only need 1-2 links) in a skillet on stove top over medium heat
- Add dash of salt, pepper, seasoning salt, and garlic salt to meat while cooking
- Add chopped green peppers, onions, and mushrooms while meat is cooking and stir ingredients together
- Crumble ground turkey or beef while cooking
- Cook meat completely through until brown
- When meat is completely cooked, use a drainer to remove excess oil from the meat
- Put meat back in a skillet and add can of tomato paste, tomato sauce, and water (12 oz to 1 cup), adding another dash of salt, pepper, seasoned salt, and garlic salt

- Cover with top and continue cooking on low for 30 – 60 minutes
- While the meat sauce is cooking, boil water in a saucepan and add 1 tablespoon of vegetable oil
- Once water begins to boil, break lasagna in half and add to water
- Allow lasagna to boil until soft
- Once the lasagna is cooked, use drainer to remove water
- Add meat sauce as the first layer to coat the casserole dish
- Add layer of lasagna
- Add layer of Meat Sauce
- Add layer of Mozzarella and American Cheese
- Repeat each set of layers 3 to 4 times
- Bake in the oven on 375 and allow cheese to melt and brown slightly
- As a short cut, substitute Ragu Spaghetti Sauce in place of onions, green peppers, mushrooms, tomato paste, tomato sauce, and water.

Recommend serving with Spinach Salad or Tossed Salad and Texas Toast

Fried Chicken

Ingredients
Pre-Cut Chicken parts
Salt
Pepper
Lawry's Seasoned Salt
All-Purpose Flour
Vegetable Oil

- Clean chicken by rinsing well with water and removing excess skin and fat
- Season chicken on all sides with Salt, Pepper, and Lawry's Seasoned Salt (Can cook immediately after seasoning or cover and refrigerate for several hours to allow seasoning to marinate into meat)
- Heat Vegetable Oil in skillet on stovetop over medium temperature
- Cover all sides of Chicken with Flour
- Once oil is hot, add chicken and allow frying for 5-7 minutes
- Once the bottom side has become golden brown, turn each piece of chicken over
- Allow chicken to cook for several minutes to become golden brown, and prick with a fork down to the bone after a few minutes to check for blood
- Turn each side of the chicken once more to ensure chicken is cooked all the way through with no signs of blood
- Once chicken is completely cooked, remove from skillet and place on plate with plain white paper towels or napkins to assist with draining excess oil

Recommend serving with Greens, Sweet Potatoes, Macaroni and Cheese, and Cornbread

Casandra Johnson

Baked Chicken or Turkey Parts

Ingredients
Pre-Cut Chicken or Turkey Parts
Salt
Pepper
Lawry's Seasoned Salt
Italian Salad Dressing or Teriyaki Sauce

➤ Clean chicken by rinsing well with water and removing excess skin and fat
➤ Season Chicken on all sides with Salt, Pepper and Seasoned Salt
➤ Place in casserole dish and use either Italian Salad Dressing or Teriyaki Sauce to pour over chicken as a marinade (Can cook immediately after seasoning or cover and refrigerate for several hours to let seasoning marinade into meat)
➤ Cover and bake in the oven on 375 for at least 1 hour
➤ Prick chicken down to the bone to ensure that blood is no longer flowing
➤ Once Chicken is completely cooked all the way through, remove the cover and allow cooking for approximately 15 – 20 additional minutes uncovered in order for chicken to brown

Can substitute chicken parts with pre-cut turkey parts, but will need to cook turkey for an additional 30 – 60 minutes

Recommend serving with Green Beans or Asparagus, Mashed Potatoes, and Brown and Serve Rolls

Barbeque Chicken

Ingredients
Pre-Cut Chicken parts
Salt
Pepper
Lawry's Seasoned Salt
Barbeque Sauce of your choice

➢ Clean chicken by rinsing well with water and removing excess skin and fat
➢ Season chicken on all sides with Salt, Pepper and Seasoned Salt (You can cook immediately after seasoning or cover and refrigerate for several hours to allow seasoning to marinate)
➢ Add just enough water to coat the pan
➢ Bake covered on 375 for at least 30 – 45 minutes
➢ Remove cover, and drain excess juice
➢ Add barbeque sauce, re-cover and put back in the oven for at least 30 minutes
➢ Prick chicken down to the bone to ensure blood is no longer flowing
➢ Once Chicken is completely cooked all the way through, remove the cover and place back in the oven for an additional 15-20 minutes uncovered in order for chicken to brown

Recommend serving with Macaroni and Cheese or Scalloped Potatoes, Green Beans, and Brown and Serve Rolls

Salmon Fillets

Ingredients
1 -2 lbs of Salmon Fillets
KC Masterpiece Honey Teriyaki with Sesame Marinade Sauce
Old Bay Seafood Seasoning

➢ Clean salmon by rinsing well with water
➢ Place salmon in a casserole dish season with Old Bay Seasoning on Both Sides
➢ Place salmon skin-side down in casserole dish
➢ Coat Salmon with Honey Teriyaki Marinade Sauce
➢ Cover and refrigerate to marinade for at least one hour
➢ Bake covered in oven on 375 for approximately 30 minutes
➢ Remove cover and allow to cook uncovered for additional 10 minutes

Also great if cooked on the grill

Recommend serving with mashed potatoes, sautéed spinach, and brown and serve rolls

Salmon Croquettes

Ingredients
1-16 oz can of Salmon
Old Bay Seasoning
1 egg
1 small onion
All-Purpose Flour
Vegetable Cooking Oil or Olive Oil

- ➤ Drain excess juice from salmon
- ➤ Put salmon in a mixing bowl
- ➤ Add a dash of Old Bay Seasoning, chopped onions, and 1 egg
- ➤ Mix ingredients extremely well
- ➤ Add coating of oil to skillet and warm on top of stove on low to medium heat
- ➤ Shape into salmon patties
- ➤ Lightly coat all sides with flour
- ➤ Put in skillet and cook to a golden brown on each side

Recommend serving with sautéed spinach and sweet potatoes or mashed potatoes

Sautéed Spinach

Ingredients
1-2 6-9 oz bags of uncooked spinach
Can of Olive Oil Spray
Chopped Garlic
Salt

- ➢ Clean spinach well by rinsing with water
- ➢ Spray skillet with coating of Olive Oil spray
- ➢ Heat skillet on stovetop over low to medium heat
- ➢ Add Spinach to skillet
- ➢ Add 1-2 tablespoons of chopped garlic
- ➢ Add dash of salt
- ➢ Stir and Cover for 3-5 minutes

Spinach Salad

Ingredients
1-2 6-9 oz bags of uncooked Spinach
1-3.75 oz bag of Honey Roasted Flavored Sliced Almonds
1 4.3 oz bag of Hormel Real Crumbled Bacon
1-2 packs of small cherry tomatoes
Red Wine Vinaigrette Salad Dressing

- ➤ Clean spinach and tomatoes very well by rinsing with water
- ➤ Mix spinach, cherry tomatoes, and ¼ to ½ bag of almonds into a bowl and toss ingredients together
- ➤ Add Salad Dressing and allow to sit in refrigerator for about an hour
- ➤ Shortly before serving, add ¼ to ½ bag of bacon bits and toss around in the salad

Casandra Johnson

Tossed Salad

Ingredients
Lettuce
Tomatoes
Cucumbers
Onions
Salad Dressing of Choice

- ➢ Clean all vegetables very well by rinsing with water
- ➢ Slice or dice vegetables to desired size
- ➢ Mix and toss vegetables together in a large bowl
- ➢ Serve with salad dressing of choice

Sautéed Asparagus

Ingredients
1/2 lb of Fresh, Raw Asparagus
Olive Oil Cooking Spray
Jar of Chopped Garlic
Salt

- Clean asparagus very well by rinsing with water
- Spray skillet with coating of Olive Oil
- Cut the ends off Asparagus
- Cut Asparagus into desired length for serving
- Add Asparagus to skillet and cook on Medium Heat
- Add teaspoon of garlic and dash of salt for seasoning
- Cover skillet and cook to desired tenderness (My personal preference is just lightly sautéed)

Casandra Johnson

Collard or Turnip Greens

Ingredients
1 lb of Fresh picked Collards or Turnip Greens or Pre-Bagged Glory Greens
Smoked Turkey Wings or Drumsticks
Salt
Crushed Red Peppers
Olive or Vegetable Cooking Oil
White Granulated Sugar

- ➢ Boil Smoked Turkey Parts in large pot of water, over medium heat, covered
- ➢ Chop and Clean Greens extremely well by soaking and rinsing several times in water
- ➢ Add greens to pot with water and smoked turkey parts
- ➢ Add 3-4 dashes of salt, 2-3 dashes of crushed red peppers, 1 teaspoon of sugar and 1 tablespoon of Olive or Vegetable Cooking Oil
- ➢ Stir in seasonings and cover while cooking over medium heat
- ➢ Turnip greens will only need to cook for 1 to 1 ½ hours, however Collard Greens will need to cook for 2 ½ to 3 hours

Green Beans

Ingredients
Fresh Green Beans
Smoked Turkey Wings or Drumsticks
Salt
Crushed Red Pepper
White Granulated Sugar
Olive or Vegetable Oil

➤ Boil Smoked Turkey Parts in large pot of water, over medium heat, covered
➤ Cut ends of green beans and clean by soaking and rinsing several times in water
➤ Cut green beans to desired length
➤ Add green beans to pot with water and smoked turkey parts
➤ Add 3-4 dashes of salt, 2-3 dashes of crushed red peppers, 1 teaspoon of Sugar and 1 Tablespoon of Olive or Vegetable Cooking Oil
➤ Stir in seasonings and cover while cooking over medium heat for approximately 1 hour or until you have desired tenderness

Casandra Johnson

Macaroni and Cheese

Ingredients
1-16 oz box of Elbow Macaroni
1 10 ¼ oz can of Campbell's Cheddar Cheese Soup
1-4 oz Can of Evaporated Milk
1-4 oz bag of grated mozzarella cheese
1-8 oz bag of grated mild cheddar cheese
1 8 oz block of sharp cheddar cheese
1 Egg
1 Tablespoon of Margarine
Salt
Pepper
Vegetable Cooking Oil
Paprika

➢ Boil water in saucepan and add a teaspoon of Vegetable Cooking Oil
➢ Once water has started boiling, add ½ box of macaroni and cook until tender
➢ Drain Water from macaroni
➢ Stir in margarine and add dash of salt and pepper
➢ Stir in ½ can of cheddar cheese soup
➢ Slice Sharp cheddar cheese and stir into macaroni
➢ Stir in ½ to ¾ contents of shredded mild Cheddar cheese and ¼ to ½ bag of shredded mozzarella cheese
➢ Beat egg and stir into macaroni along with evaporated milk
➢ Once contents are all mixed well, transfer ingredients to casserole dish
➢ Sprinkle layer of shredded mild cheddar cheese over top of macaroni and cheese dish
➢ Sprinkle a light coating of Paprika across the top of dish

➤ Bake uncovered in oven on 375 for approximately 20-30 minutes, checking periodically for browning and also pricking an area of the dish with a fork to ensure macaroni and cheese is cooked all the way through

Mashed Potatoes

Ingredients
3-4 Fresh potatoes
1-4oz can of evaporated milk
Margarine
Garlic Salt or chopped garlic
Salt
Pepper

- Clean potatoes very well by rinsing and soaking in water
- Boil potatoes on stove top in water with skin on
- Boil until potatoes become soft
- Drain water from potatoes
- You can either leave the skin on or peel it off (skin will peel right off) – I personally prefer to just remove some of the skin, but not all
- Mash potatoes with large spoon or mashing utensil
- Stir in dash of salt and pepper
- Stir in dash of garlic salt or teaspoon of chopped garlic
- Stir in 3-4 teaspoons of margarine
- Stir in ½ to full can of Evaporated milk – (Ensuring not to make it too soupy)
- Mix all ingredients in well until potatoes become smooth and creamy
- Cook on top of stove on low to medium heat until there is consistency

Potato Salad

Ingredients
3-4 potatoes
2-3 eggs
1 small onion
1 small green pepper
Sweet Relish
Miracle Whip
Yellow Mustard
Salt
Pepper
Celery Salt
Paprika

➢ Clean potatoes very well by rinsing and soaking in water
➢ Boil potatoes on stovetop with skin on in water
➢ Boil until potatoes become soft, but not mushy
➢ While potatoes are boiling, chop onions and green peppers into small, fine pieces
➢ Boil eggs
➢ Once potatoes are finished cooking, drain hot water and run cool water over them so they are not too hot to touch
➢ Peel skin from potatoes (skin will come right off potatoes)
➢ Once eggs are boiled, drain hot water and run cool water over them so they are not too hot to touch
➢ Remove shell from eggs
➢ Chop potatoes and eggs and mix together in a large bowl
➢ Add onions, green peppers, and relish with potatoes and eggs
➢ Add miracle whip and mustard to give yellow color
➢ Stir ingredients together really well, adding in pinch of salt, pepper, and celery salt

➢ Transfer mixed potato salad to a large bowl and sprinkle dash of paprika across the top

Scalloped Potatoes

Ingredients
3-4 Potatoes
1 small onion
Milk
Margarine
8 oz bag of Grated Mild Cheddar Cheese
8 oz block of Sharp Cheddar Cheese
Salt
Pepper
Paprika

➢ Clean potatoes very well by rinsing and soaking in water
➢ Peel skin and slice potatoes based on desired size
➢ Slice onions and add to potatoes
➢ Add milk, several slices of margarine, ½ to ¾ contents of grated mild cheddar cheese, and ½ contents of sliced sharp cheddar cheese
➢ Stir ingredients together and add in a dash of salt and pepper
➢ Transfer mixed ingredients to casserole dish
➢ Spread a layer of shredded mild cheddar cheese on top
➢ Sprinkle dash of paprika across the top
➢ Cover dish and bake in oven on 375 for approximately 60 minutes or until desired tenderness is reached
➢ Remove cover and place in oven for approximately 10 minutes to allow browning

Sweet Potatoes

Ingredients
3-4 Fresh Sweet Potatoes
White Granulated Sugar
Margarine
8 oz can of Pineapple Chunks
Vanilla Flavoring (Pure or Imitation)
Nutmeg
Cinnamon
Water

➢ Clean sweet potatoes very well by rinsing and soaking in water
➢ Peel skin
➢ Cut potatoes into slices or small pieces
➢ Place potatoes in saucepan
➢ Add ¾ to 1 full cup of sugar
➢ Add ¼ to ½ stick of margarine
➢ Add can of pineapple chunks with juice
➢ Add tablespoon of vanilla flavoring, and 2-3 dashes of nutmeg and cinnamon
➢ Add enough water to ensure potatoes are completely immersed in water
➢ Cover saucepan, place on baking pan and place in oven on 375 for approximately 1 to 1 ½ hours
➢ Remove top and allow to continue baking while uncovered for 30 – 45 minutes

Yellow Squash

Ingredients
3-4 Fresh Yellow Squash
1 small onion
Salt
Pepper
Sugar
Olive Oil Cooking Spray

➢ Clean squash very well by rinsing and soaking in water
➢ Cut off both ends of the squash
➢ Leave skin on and slice remaining squash to desired size
➢ Slice onion
➢ Spray coating of olive oil in skillet
➢ Add squash and onions to skillet and cook on stovetop over medium heat
➢ Add dash of salt, pepper, and sugar
➢ Place top over skillet and allow to cook for approximately 15 minutes or until desired tenderness is reached
➢ Remove cover and allow to continue cooking uncovered for 3-5 minutes to allow browning if desired

Casandra Johnson

Homemade Burgers

Ingredients
1lb pack of Ground Turkey or Beef
1 small onion
1 small green pepper
Salt
Pepper
Lawry's Seasoned Salt
Cheese - Optional
Lettuce
Tomato
Sandwich Buns

➢ Chop onion and green pepper into small pieces
➢ Put Ground Turkey or Beef in a large mixing bowl
➢ Add chopped onions and green peppers
➢ Add a dash of salt, pepper, and seasoned salt
➢ Mix ingredients really well
➢ Shape mixture into patties
➢ Warm skillet on stovetop over medium heat
➢ If making turkey burgers, coat skillet with layer of olive oil cooking spray
➢ Add burgers ensuring there is appropriate space between each patty
➢ Allow each side to cook until patties have become brown on the bottom and half way through actual burger
➢ Ensure burger is cooked all the way through – Can test by ensuring there is no blood flowing and juices are clear
➢ Once the burger is cooked all the way through, remove and drain excess oil
➢ If adding cheese, place on top of burger immediately after removing from skillet to allow cheese to melt

➢ Serve on sandwich buns with slices of lettuce, tomatoes, and condiments of you r choice.

➢ Recommend serving with homemade French fries
➢ In place of using skillet, can also use George Foreman grill

Casandra Johnson

Homemade French Fries

Ingredients
3-4 potatoes
Vegetable, Olive, or Peanut Oil
Salt or Lawry's Seasoned Salt

➤ Clean potatoes very well by rinsing and soaking with water
➤ Peel skin from potatoes, if desired (I personally prefer to leave some of the skin on)
➤ Cut potatoes into desired French fry size
➤ Heat oil of choice in a large saucepan or frying pot over medium heat
➤ Once oil becomes hot, add French fries
➤ Allow French fries to cook all the way through until golden brown and desired tenderness is reached
➤ Used draining utensil to remove French fries from cooking oil
➤ Drain excess oil by placing over plain napkins or paper towels
    ➤ Season with salt or seasoned salt to desired taste

Fried Bologna Sandwich – One of my favorite Classics!

Ingredients
8oz pack of Oscar Mayer Bologna with the red wrapping
Sliced yellow American cheese
Fresh loaf of bread
Mustard
Margarine

- ➢ Add 1-2 teaspoons of margarine to a skillet and heat on stovetop over medium heat
- ➢ Remove red wrapping from around the bologna
- ➢ Once the margarine has melted, add slice of bologna to the skillet
- ➢ Cook over medium heat until the center of the bologna rises
- ➢ Turn bologna over and cook on the opposite side until the center rises to the top
- ➢ Add slice of cheese on top of bologna, allowing cheese to melt
- ➢ Place cooked bologna and cheese on top of a slice of bread, adding mustard over the top of the bologna
- ➢ Place 2nd slice of bread on top to make a complete sandwich
- ➢ Cut Sandwich in half and serve with Frito's Corn Chips and an iced cold glass of Iced-Tea with lemon

Casandra Johnson

Fresh Squeezed Lemonade

Ingredients
2-3 Fresh Lemons
White Granulated Sugar
Water

➤ Cut each lemon in half
➤ Squeeze juice from each lemon into a quart sized pitcher
➤ Add 1 cup of sugar to squeezed lemon juice
➤ Slice each lemon and add to pitcher
➤ Fill pitcher with cold water, stirring mixture together very well
➤ Serve lemonade in a glass, with or without ice

Sweet Iced Tea with Lemon

2 Lipton's family-sized Tea Bags
2 Lemons
White Granulated Sugar
Water
Ice

➢ Boil tea bags in 2-3 cups of water in medium sized sauce pan
➢ Fill quart-sized pitcher with ice
➢ Add 1 cup of sugar to pitcher
➢ Once tea bags have come to a boil, remove bags and pour hot tea into pitcher
➢ Cut each lemon in half
➢ Squeeze juice from each lemon into pitcher
➢ Slice each lemon and add to pitcher
➢ Stir mixture extremely well, adding more ice if all of the previous ice has melted and in order for there to be a full pitcher of tea
➢ Serve sweet iced tea with lemon in a glass, with or without additional ice

Casandra Johnson

𝔄𝔣𝔱𝔢𝔯𝔴𝔬𝔯𝔡 𝔟𝔶 𝔈𝔯𝔦𝔠 𝔍𝔢𝔯𝔬𝔪𝔢 𝔇𝔦𝔠𝔨𝔢𝔶

Back before Webster went insane and words like Bootylicious made it into the dictionary,

Back when we were black and proud...

Back when music was played on radio stations around the world without every other word being bleeped...

Afros and bell bottoms were the clothing we wore to our private Woodstock,

Back when there was no Internet so people had to talk, and you didn't click a button on a social website and make someone you've never met and probably never will see be your "friend",

Back then friends were people you actually knew by sight and when talking, you didn't type your words into a box; you heard the sounds of their voices, you knew your friend's voice like it was your favorite song. You didn't log on to see your "friends" but you knocked on doors and when they greeted you, you saw their expressions, you shared Kool-Aid and emotions, not bogus "Cyber" drinks and meaningless emoticons...

That was back in the day.

Eric Jerome Dickey – New York Times Best Selling Author

Remember Back in the Day

About the Author

Casandra Johnson is the President and Founder of Kingdom Journey Enterprises, which has been created to empower, inspire, equip, and connect world class leaders for ministry and the marketplace. She was raised in the Washington, DC area where she grew up in the church and accepted her call to ministry at a young age, and was later licensed as a Minister while serving at New Life Anointed Ministries in Woodbridge, VA. Prior to taking the leap of faith to start Kingdom Journey Enterprises, Casandra enjoyed a successful career that spanned from serving on Active Duty Military, the Federal Government and with Lockheed Martin and Booz Allen Hamilton. Casandra has earned a Bachelor's of Science Degree in Business Management from George Mason University and a Master's of Art Degree in Biblical Studies from Beulah Heights University.

Casandra is a National Best Selling Author with two previous titles to her credit to include "Free to Live Again" and "Dear Daddy: Remembering Him, Discovering Me", as well as she has been a contributing writer for numerous published works by other authors. Casandra's testimony is that she loves God with all her heart, mind, and soul, and she would not trade anything for her life's journey. She has one daughter, Brittany.

To learn more information or to contact Casandra Johnson for book signings, to be a guest speaker or lecturer for your upcoming event, or to schedule media interviews, visit www.casandrajohnson.com or send your request by e-mail to kingdomjourney@aol.com.

A FULL-SERVICE PUBLISHING COMPANY

Kingdom Journey Press, Inc. is a full-service publishing company which provides customized services to support our clients from the conception of an idea to getting HIStory to the masses! Since the time of inception and in conjunction with its umbrella organization, Kingdom Journey Enterprises, we have become recognized globally for our ability to establish a unique presence, while building relationships with partners and clients consisting of current and aspiring authors, and ministry, business, and community organizations.

Our services include:

- ➢ Manuscript Evaluation
- ➢ Coaching for current and aspiring authors
- ➢ Editing
- ➢ Print and Electronic Media
- ➢ National Distribution
- ➢ Marketing, Public Relations, and Sales Support

To learn more about our services, we invite you to visit us on-line at www.kjpressinc.com.

www.ingramcontent.com/pod-product-compliance
Lightning Source LLC
LaVergne TN
LVHW011207080426
835508LV00007B/643